Justice and Joy

Mindfulness in Social and Political Activism

Table of Contents

Chapter 1. Introduction

Step into a realm where passion meets serenity, in our illuminating Special Report: "Justice and Joy: Mindfulness in Social and Political Activism". Dive in as we explore the extraordinary crossroad where keen consciousness and ardent activism converge, challenging our accustomed perspectives. This vibrant report unravels how mindfulness can fuel social and political activism, making it an even more potent tool for change in our increasingly connected world. It's a captivating fusion of societal urgency and inner tranquility that will surely enlighten, inspire, and compel you to take a proactive role in shaping our shared future. So spark your curiosity, ignite your enthusiasm, and join us on this profound journey of justice, joy, and the power of being present. Are you ready to make a mindful difference? This Special Report is just the beginning.

Chapter 2. Awakening: Understanding the Intersection of Mindfulness and Activism

The cornerstone of any transformative shift in society resides in the understanding of self. To bring about a change, activists across the world are increasingly turning towards mindfulness. This introspective practice, often associated with calm and tranquility, might initially seem at odds with the dynamic and demanding realm of social activism. But, on closer inspection, there is a remarkable affinity between the two, creating a resilient intersection that is both potent and liberating.

2.1. The Core of Mindfulness

Mindfulness is essentially rooted in the present moment. It invites us to deeply immerse ourselves in the current, flowing rhythm of life, to cultivate an intimate awareness of our thoughts, feelings, sensations, and surrounding environment. It transcends the constraints of judgment or bias, ushering us into a space of acceptance and understanding.

This core principle of mindfulness does more than just fostering inner peace. It also unveils our linked existence, helping us comprehend the intrinsic interconnectivity between ourselves and the world. This realization cultivates empathy, compassion, and understanding - fundamental traits needed for effective social and political activism.

2.2. Harmonizing Personal and Social Transformation

Social and political activism strives to alter systems, shift ideologies, and challenge the status quo. These macro changes, however, begin at the micro level. It is through individual transformations that collective change gets triggered. Consequently, the personal growth and awareness brought forth by mindfulness become quintessential for broader societal transformation.

Mindful activists choose actions motivated by love, empathy, and understanding instead of anger and frustration. These conscious actions can be as contagious as they are beneficial, having the potential to invoke and propagate systemic transformations.

2.3. The Activist's Advantage: Emotional Resilience

Being at the front lines of social and political battles can be exhausting. Activists consistently face opposition, critique, and indifference, which might lead to burnout and apathy. Here, mindfulness practices bestow an enduring resilience, enabling activists to maintain composure, patience, and most importantly, hope, in the face of adversity. It also equips them with the ability to manage emotions effectively, ensuring that responses are mindful rather than reactive.

This resilience also lets activists plan their endeavors wisely. They become more observant of political landscapes, social nuances, and most importantly, their own mental health. Gaining such emotional balance and clarity, they can chart paths that are not just passionate, but also pragmatic for effective activism.

2.4. Walking the Path: Techniques and Practice

Just as there are a multitude of ways to approach activism, there are also numerous mindfulness techniques adjusted to different preferences and lifestyles. Regular meditation, yoga, focused breathing, journaling, and even mindful walking are some commonly used techniques. The methods may vary, but the core remains the same – being completely present and psychologically immersed in the current activity.

2.5. Bringing It All Together: Mindful Actions for Change

In the apparent dichotomy of tranquility and urgency, the fusion of mindfulness and activism emerges as a uniquely compelling force. Mindful actions, developed through compassion, understanding, and humility, will serve to enhance the efficacy of social and political activism.

When the activist's vision of a better world is harmoniously integrated with the soothing essence of mindfulness, the potential to bring about impactful change becomes endless. Wisdom and compassion, action and patience, strength and resilience, the seemingly divergent traits coalesce to form the mindful activist - an agent of transformation embracing both the turmoil of the world and tranquility of the self.

So, as we delve into mindfulness's impact on activism, remember, this journey is about introspection as much as it is about external change. That every thoughtful pause, every calming breath, and every present moment aids in building a more compassionate, equitable, and just world. Such is the power of the intersection between mindfulness and activism, and this awakening could be the dawn of a revolution.

Chapter 3. From Self to Society: Personal Transformation to Structural Change

In order to weave the transformation from personal change to broad structural evolution, we first need to understand the profound concept of mindfulness and its impact at a personal level. Once we realize how mindfulness can craft individual resilience and empathy, we can then fathom its potential to inspire collective change.

3.1. The Notion of Mindfulness

Mindfulness, at its core, is the intentional focus on the present moment without judgement. It calls for the acknowledgement of thoughts, emotions, and sensations as they arise, enabling one to respond with patience rather than react impulsively. While often associated with serenity and tranquility, the fruits of mindfulness go beyond calmness. It enhances self-awareness, fortifies mental resilience, and fosters empathy — traits paramount for personal transformation. This understanding, when translated into actions, forms the foundation for social activism.

3.2. Personal Transformation through Mindfulness

Mindfulness uncovers a path to personal transformation by fostering self-awareness and fronting one's emotional intelligence. It allows you to delve deep into your thoughts, unconscious biases, assumptions, and behaviors. This process of introspection cultivates self-understanding, essential for any substantial personal growth.

Moreover, mindfulness teaching involves ethics and compassion as fundamental elements. Through mindfulness, individuals learn to circumnavigate their reactions and instead respond mindfully to challenging circumstances. This behavioral tweak yields resilience, allowing one to face societal or individual issues with courage and arise as an advocate for change.

3.3. Empathy: The Common Thread

Empathy is an essential byproduct of mindful practice. It allows the exposure to perspectives outside one's immediate existence, transcending the personal sphere into collective consciousness. Understanding others' experiences, concerns, and trials back one's incentive to alleviate this collective suffering. Thus, empathy, driven by mindfulness, operates as a bridge to social activism.

3.4. Mindfulness as a Stepping Stone to Social Activism

The coupling of self-understanding, resilience, and empathy prepares a fertile ground for social activism. Mindful individuals can empathize with the grievances of marginalized communities and channel their own resilience to bring about equitable change. Fighting for social justice can feel overwhelming; mindfulness assures us that change is incremental, every action matters, and resilience will overcome setbacks.

3.5. Structural Change: The Culmination Point

The power of relentless individuals collectively advocating for change can drive structural evolution. Mindful activism supports problem-solving that is aware, compassionate, inclusive, and respects the intricacies of the system in question. Such an approach detects systemic issues at their roots, enabling sustainable change rather than tackling mere symptoms.

It's essential to acknowledge that widespread transformation is not an instant shift, but a gradual process over time. The consistency and vigor of mindful activists contribute to a momentum that can slowly but definitively alter the face of society.

As we embark on the path of personal transformation through mindfulness, we illuminate a trail of structural change that leads to equity and justice. Mindfulness assists us in recognizing our interconnectedness with all beings. The realization that our liberation is tied to the liberation of all seeds the genesis of mindful social activism. Breaking the shackles of indifference and nurturing compassion, mindfulness takes us from self to society, creating ripples of resilient change in the world around us.

Chapter 4. Activism Reimagined: The Role of Inner Calm Amidst the Turmoil

In an era of relentless upheaval and social transformation, the role of inner tranquility often gets cloaked under the voluminous intensity of public participation. However, for the sustainable efficacy of activism, it's essential to develop a paradoxical alliance with silence, calm and mindfulness, as serenity's part in activism is not simply supportive, it's foundational.

4.1. The Centrality of Inner Calm

The basis to all activism is the decisively resolute and unyielding belief in change, coupled with an unquenchable thirst to streamline societal mechanisms. However, experiencing this impetus amidst the tumultuous waves of societal shifts could be exhausting, causing burn-out. This is where the principle of inner calm, gained through mindfulness, steps in. It equips activists with the stamina and resilience required for the long struggle for social justice.

The centrality of inner calm in activism emphasizes the need for self-care and the cultivation of emotional resilience. Mindfulness practice, designed to draw our attention to the present moment and develop an attitude of acceptance, can promote this stamina, building a robust emotional and psychological framework that bolsters activists against potential burnout.

4.2. Mindfulness and Activism: An Unlikely Duo

Contrary to popular belief, mindfulness and activism are not antagonistic domains; instead, they are two facets of a holistic approach to societal transformation. The marriage of the two is a testament to the inherent strength of an activist fueled by an awareness that maintains an equanimity regardless of external circumstances. This level of conscientious engagement, deeply rooted in empathy, projects an inwardly calm activist who is effective in demanding, achieving, and maintaining groundbreaking societal transformations.

Moreover, mindfulness allows activists to become more perceptive to the subtleties of societal injustices. By cultivating an open and receptive mind, activists can grasp a fuller understanding of the societal and political landscapes – an understanding that remains undistorted by personal biases.

4.3. The Transformative Power of Mindful Activism

A close look at mindful activism reveals how it can transform not only the individual activist, but also the entire landscape of social and political activism. When activism is pursued with a mindful approach, it evolves from a mere reaction to societal issues into a carefully considered, empathetic engagement that listens before it speaks and understands before it demands.

Mindful activism also presents an antidote to divisive, inflammatory, and alienating methods of protest. Instead of drawing lines between 'us' versus 'them', mindful activism seeks to understand and empathize with oppositional standpoints, and in doing so, it paves the way for dialogue, connection, and mutual understanding.

The adoption of mindfulness into the activist realm empowers individuals to navigate the emotionally charged sphere of societal justice with peace, authenticity, and unwavering dedication. It allows activists to unweariedly champion the cause, keeping the flame of passion alive yet preventing the exhaustion that could result from an impulsive, aggressive approach.

4.4. Infusing Inner Calm in Activist Practices

To weave mindfulness into the fabric of activism, it's essential for activists to cultivate personal spaces for reflection and introspection, often through mediation or other mindful practices. Daily routines might encompass stillness and breathing practices, promoting equanimity and a balanced response to societal ordeals.

Similarly, advocacy groups could host facilitated group meditations and mindfulness sessions focusing on interconnectedness, compassion, and communal healing. Incorporating such practices affords a reason to press pause, fill up one's own reservoir, and enables an individual to continue to partake in the inevitably protracted journey of activism.

4.5. The Never-Ending Journey: Activism and Continuous Mindfulness

While mindfulness endows us with the power to elevate our activist efforts, its practice calls for perseverance and consistency. Just as societal change is not a one-off endeavor, mindfulness is a long-term engagement that demands a continuous commitment.

As much as the characteristics of inner calm and mindfulness may seem antithetical to the typical image of a vehement activist, these are the very traits that can render activism more sustainable and effective. By committing to the pursuit of inner peace amidst the turmoil, we choose to defy conventional activism and contribute to a movement that is resilient and robust, fueled by an enduring sense of passion and stamina that refuses to extinguish.

Implementing mindfulness requires determined effort, but its boundless benefits both on personal and communal levels render it a worthwhile pursuit. By prioritizing inner calm and mental clarity, we can navigate the tumultuous yet exhilarating journey of activism with an unwavering commitment to societal betterment. Thus, inner calm doesn't act as a barrier to the outcry for justice; instead, it transforms it into a more sustainable, empathetic, and effective endeavor, contributing to a profound revolutionizing of activism as we know it.

Harnessing the power of mindfulness for activism is indeed a reimagining of the quintessential activist archetype - replacing heated passion with enlightened passion, tumultuous outcry with potent silence, and exhaustion with sustainability. It's about changing the 'how' of activism, to ensure the 'whys' can drive us further and deeper into the pursuit of justice and equality. Activism is indeed reimagined when the tranquility within balances the chaos without.

Chapter 5. The Joyful Warrior: Harnessing Happiness in the Pursuit of Social Justice

In this unfathomable journey towards societal betterment, a new breed of activist has emerged, imbued with an outlook—one that strategically molds joy, happiness, and mindfulness into an impactful tool for change. These activists, colloquially referred to as the Joyful Warriors, seek equity, social justice, and freedom, not through rage or incessant conflict, but through a potent amalgam of boundless joy, profound mindfulness, and relentless resolve.

5.1. Embracing Joy as Activism

Often, one might conjure an image of activism adorned with anger, rebellion, and strenuous confrontation. However, the most impactful activism transcends wrath and incites changes with a smile, an approach where joy and passion underpin the drive to transform society. Happiness and cheerfulness aren't trivial luxuries for the fortunate few but imperative tools that inspire and fortify activists in their continued pursuit of concrete socio-political change. Nurturing a sense of joy in the midst of social activism helps with condensing complex issues into palatable dialogues, encouraging a broader audience to engage in hard discussions readily, and carrying on change-making conversations in a compelling, transformative, and inviting way.

5.2. Joy as a Form of Resistance

Historically, people have found solace in joy and happiness in the face of adversity. For centuries, marginalized communities have harnessed the power of joy as an act of defiance and a testament to their resilience. Joy presents itself as a form of resistance—a silent insurgence against oppressive frameworks intent on stifling our spirits. It acts as a beacon that illuminates the path for others, reminding us of the potential for bliss amidst tumult and the happiness that can bloom even amid despair.

5.3. Mindfulness Meets Activism

Here, the practice of mindfulness emerges as a crucial ally. By promoting an acute awareness of our inner emotional state and encouraging an accepting, non-judgmental perspective towards our feelings, mindfulness allows us to balance the spectrum of emotions experienced during activism. Activists practicing mindfulness can channel their anger, frustration, and fear adequately without losing touch with the driving forces of hope, love, and joy. Through mindfulness, the Joyful Warrior learns to find peace in chaos, serenity in struggle, and resilience in adversity.

5.4. Replenishing the Spirit with Joy

Continually advocating for change can be depleting. Persistent battles against systemic injustices often entail emotional toll. Amid such challenges, it's paramount to find and replenish the joy necessary to sustain oneself for the long haul of activism. Moments of gratitude, love, and happiness should not merely be sought after; they should be created, to fuel the spirit in moments of despair. By integrating mindfulness practices with constant efforts to nurture joy, activists can develop a resilient spirit that holds steadily even during the grimmest periods.

5.5. The Power of Positive Energy

A positive frame of mind not only affects the individual activist but also influences the social dynamics around the cause. The energy that one emanates greatly molds the narrative surrounding the movement. A peaceful protest led by joy, for instance, may attract contrasting reactions and engagements from authority and bystanders compared to an angry march. The Joyful Warrior, thus, understands the profound power of positive energy in drawing attention and engaging those who may initially be disconnected or opposed, subsequently building empathy, understanding, and allyship.

5.6. Inclusive Happiness

In building a community, an integral objective is fostering a sense of belonging. As we engage others in difficult discussions, it's crucial not only to share the pain but also to remember to share the joy. Celebrating victories, big or small, fosters a sense of unity, encourages continued engagement, ignites hope, and — perhaps most importantly — humanizes the struggle. Finding and sharing happiness make the journey appealing, showing that social activism is not solely about fighting; it is about growing together, caring deeply, and creating a compassionate world for all.

5.7. Conclusion

In conclusion, the Joyful Warrior treads a path of activism that is rich with emotional intelligence, deep mindfulness, and a pervasive sense of joy. Harnessing happiness in the pursuit of social justice empowers activists to maintain resilience, engage a broader audience, and energize the movement. The joyful pursuit of justice, therefore, constitutes a robust form of activism—a path that elicits change not merely by battling what is wrong, but also by celebrating what is or can be right, and instilling that hope into the heart of our collective consciousness. It is in this spirit that we urge you to seek the cultivation of joy, to find your calm in the storm, and to be the Joyful Warrior that illuminely advances in the face of adversity.

Chapter 6. Mindfulness as a Catalyst: Enhancing Empathy and Compassiveness

Mindfulness is the practice of being fully present, grounded, and engaged in each moment, a skill cultivated through various techniques like meditation, conscious breathing, or mindful movement, such as yoga. This practice helps enhance our empathy and compassion, creating a ripple effect in all aspects of our life—personal, professional, and importantly, in our societal engagements.

6.1. Mindfulness and Empathy: The Perceptual Shift

At its core, empathy is the capacity to understand and share the feelings of others, indeed an essential tool for human connection. Through mindfulness, we can enhance our empathic capabilities by deepening a profound awareness of the present moment.

Mindfulness nudges our attention towards the full panorama of our experiences. We regain the ability to perceive and understand our daily encounters without the habitual response patterns clouded by our biases. This perceptual shift highlights the interconnectivity of all beings, facilitating a deeper comprehension of shared human experiences, that is essential for empathy.

Consider yourself walking down a bustling street, perhaps rushing off to work. As you navigate through the crowd, you likely overlook the faces you pass. It's an unusual scenario for intentional mindfulness, yet, in this setting, mindfulness means slowing your internal pace, observing, and tuning into the feelings and lives unfolding around you. The thrum of human activity becomes a symphony of shared emotions and experiences. With firm empathy, we can connect with these experiences deeply rather than dismiss them as background noise.

6.2. Mindfulness: Cultivating Compassion

Equally impactful is the role mindfulness plays in fostering compassion, an emotional response elicited when perceiving suffering and coupled with an authentic desire to alleviate it. Unlike empathy, compassion takes the experience a step further towards an intention for intervention, which, in a social and political activism context, is crucial.

For many, recognizing suffering, let alone wanting to relieve it, is challenging. Compassion involves crossing the self-imposed boundaries of comfort, bred by fear or indifference. This is where mindfulness becomes instrumental.

Traditional mindfulness techniques focus on generating a compassionate response in the practitioner. For instance, Loving Kindness Meditation or Metta Bhavana involves silently repeating phrases of kindness, like "May you be happy. May you be well," first towards oneself, and then expanding the circle to include loved ones, neutral individuals, difficult people, and ultimately, all sentient beings.

The practice helps cultivate an internal environment of compassion, initiating a positive feedback loop. As we experience compassion for others, our inner reservoir of kindness expands, further empowering us to stir pools of compassion for those around us.

6.3. The Symbiosis of Mindfulness, Empathy, and Compassion

Both empathy and compassion are developed and enhanced through mindfulness. There is an interdependence and flow between these three components, creating a nourishing cycle—mindfulness amplifies empathy, empathy fosters compassion, and compassion informs mindful actions.

Through a sustained mindfulness practice, one gradually constructs a harmonious balance between empathy and compassion. Feeling the pain of others without the motivating drive to help can be draining and lead to empathy fatigue. Balanced with compassion, though, we not only share the emotions of those suffering but also gain the strength to act against it.

This balance helps activists sustain their efforts, preventing compassion fatigue or burnout, often attributed to the emotionally demanding nature of activism. Activists can maintain resilience while responding effectively to social and political issues.

6.4. Activating Social and Political Change

In the theatre of social and political activism, mindfulness, empathy, and compassion manifest as a unifying force. They foster an attitude of persistence, patience, and non-judging that underpin any successful movement.

Each moment of mindfulness imbues the activists with a sense of purpose and clarity, encouraging them to face disturbing truths, withstand subjugation, and persist in the face of distress. Empathy and compassion, on the other hand, strengthen the cause, inspiring collaborative action to lift collective suffering.

Adequately equipped with empathy and compassion, activists can then challenge inhumane practices, co-create solutions, and mobilize communities effectively. They become emotionally agile leaders who can turn differences into strength and division into unity.

6.5. Woven into Practice: Case Studies

At this juncture, concrete examples can best illuminate the unfolding of mindfulness in amplifying empathy and compassion within social and political activism.

An informative case would be Compassion In Action, a conflict resolution organization. They leverage mindfulness to boost empathetic communication, aiding individuals in conflict-ridden regions to bridge divides. Moreover, their 'Compassionate Listening Project' trains activists to listen empathetically, a vital tool to deescalate the chaos in their surroundings.

On a larger scale, political figures like Congressman Tim Ryan have begun advocating for incorporating mindfulness in governmental institutions. In his book 'A Mindful Nation', Ryan underscores the transformative power that mindfulness, empathy, and compassion can wield in policy creation and implementation.

Such examples concretely highlight how mindfulness catalyzes empathy and compassion, helping make a deep impact in our interconnected world.

In conclusion, mindfulness serves as a powerful catalyst for enhancing empathy and compassion, and thus becomes integral to social and political activism. Not only does it equip individuals with tools for personal growth but also empowers communities at large to socially and politically engage with heightened empathy and compassion, driving meaningful change.

Chapter 7. Meditation and Movements: The Silent Strength Behind Loud Calls

In the throes of a chaotic world churning ceaselessly with disparate voices, the concept of tranquil meditation converging with mellifluous social movements seems paradoxical. Yet, the heart of hope beating steadily within this paradox illuminates a powerful path forward. It is where the strength burgeoned from internal peace bolsters the loud calls that challenge oppressive norms. This chapter excavates the link between individual and collective consciousness, reflected in and propelled by the act of meditation, and their impact on socio-political activism.

7.1. The Power of Silent Dedication

At the heart of every social movement lies a passion for change, a drive for justice, and an impenetrable will that stems from deep, personal convictions. These convictions, however subjective or universal, carry discernible strength. But can there be power in silence? Can discarding words and embracing quiet introspection feed a clamor for change?

The practice of meditation brings this query to life. When we meditate, we discover our capacity to delve deep into an ocean of inner calm and resurface with pearls of clarity and understanding. It lets us disentangle from the chaos outside, helping us refine our focus and fortify our resolve. By providing an avenue to navigate our inner landscape, meditation uncovers reservoirs of resilience, allowing activists to balance energy and mitigate emotional exhaustion, a common demon in any fight for justice.

7.2. The Intersection of Meditation and Activism

Situated at the intersection of introspective silence and vocal advocacy, we find a space for mindful activism. But what does mindfulness mean within an activist context? Therein lies the transformative power of meditation, as it deftly bridges the individual and the collective.

Mindfulness, in its simplest form, is the cultivation of conscious awareness. Within activism, this means maintaining a purposeful presence amidst prevailing turbulence. It helps activists remain resolute in their cause without getting lost or overwhelmed by the magnanimity of overarching societal crises. As grassroots organizations and NGOs worldwide have started harnessing the power of mindful meditation, they've found it to be a tool not only for relaxation and personal growth but also for fostering empathy, collaboration, and resilience amongst their members.

7.3. Case Studies: Meditation in Major Movements

Meditation has unexpectedly emerged as an indispensable tool in some of the century's most significant social and political protests. From the Civil Rights Movement to the protests against climate change, let's overview few of these phenomenal instances.

1. Civil Rights Movement: The Civil Rights Movement saw the application of Mahatma Gandhi's principles of non-violent resistance transplanted to American soil. Gandhi's own practices were profoundly influenced by inner discipline and self-awareness stemming from meditation. Leaders like Martin Luther King Jr. further perpetuated Gandhi's teachings of peace, empathy, and steadfast resolve, strengthened by meditation.

2. Climate Activism: The Sunrise Movement and Extinction Rebellion, prominent organizations in the fight against climate change, incorporate meditation in their protests. These moments of collective, intentional silence help them refocus, re-energize, and reaffirm their commitment to the cause.

As we meticulously dissect these movements and others, it becomes evident that meditation has not only been a supplemental force but a cornerstone guiding activists to envision innovative ways of enacting societal change.

7.4. The Challenges and Potential Solutions

While mindful meditation shows promise for empowering activism, challenges remain. Naysayers question its effectiveness in a context so practical, urgent, and external. However, even these skeptics cannot deny the growing burnout and compassion fatigue affecting many activists. It is within these very struggles that we uncover the importance of an activist's internal landscape.

The key, then, in merging meditation with activism lies in promoting a shift in perspective - emphasizing that such practice isn't a detour from the path to change but an essential gear in the activist's machine. Psychological wellness initiatives, mindfulness training, and intentional quiet moments at protests all pave a way toward incorporating meditation, thus fortifying the activist spirit.

7.5. Forward Momentum

Just as a whisper can still the most cacophonous storm, the silent strength fostered by meditation can fortify loud calls for societal transformation. As we recognize and appreciate this unique amalgamation, we move towards a new era of activism — one that is not just about shouting against the oppressors but also about healing the oppressed.

May the journey into our beings and the reflection upon the collective conscience through meditation not only fortify our voices but also amplify the silence between the words we speak. As social and political activism continues to weave its narrative in our global society stories, may we remember to turn inward as much as we push outward, creating spaces of justice fueled by joy, and form movements shaped not just by loud calls, but by their silent strengths too.

Chapter 8. Inner Peace, Global Impact: The Rippling Effect of Mindful Activism

In the ceaseless flurry of today's world, the concept of mindfulness, whether it's hammered out on a yoga mat, within quiet contemplation, or shaped through dynamic interaction, has become an instrumental factor of how we perceive our surrounding environment, and more significantly, how we choose to engage with it. Thus unfolds the intricate fabric of mindful activism, steming from a deeply personal resolve and blossoming into a universal call for change.

8.1. The Genesis of Mindful Activism

For most of us, opening our mental diaries to the word 'activism', images of streets filled with placards, fiery speeches, and organised demonstrations leap forth. Conversely, 'mindfulness' casts us in the tranquility of meditative practices, a silence reverberating within, and a calming resonance with the self.

And yet, beyond the surface dichotomy, these two forces are not only compatible; they can work synergistically to create spaces for internal peace and external justice. Mindful activism is about bringing your full presence, awareness, and compassion into the world, using your actions to promote positive change.

"Mindful activism is more than a political act; it's a holistic practice — a lived manifesta of one's values and a harmonious accord between one's aspirations for the world and one's inner state of being."

8.2. The Intersection of Inner Tranquility and External Resilience

Drawing from the deep reservoirs of self-awareness and keen cognizance that are part and parcel of mindfulness, one imbues their actions with thoughtful deliberation, compassion, and a rootedness in their quest for change, making their activism less of an impulsive reaction and more of a purposeful action.

This intersection between the tranquility of a mindful being and the resilient force of activism acts as a potent catalyst of transformation. It harmonizes the discourse between the activist in ourselves, clamouring for external justice, and the mindful custodian of our emotions, advocating for inner calm.

"Both mindfulness and activism are virtues of the brave — audacious in the surrender to serenity and valiant in the face of systemic adversities. Together, they become an unstoppable force."

8.3. Cultivating the Roots of Mindful Activism

There is no one-size-fits-all method to cultivating mindful activism, but it might begin simply with spending time in contemplation or meditation, acknowledging the truths of our reality and the injustices that need addressing. Through this practice, one raises their empathy quotient, harnessing this emotional intelligence to act more carefully, inclusively, and thoroughly.

It also involves listening — not just with our ears but with an openness that extends beyond physical presences. The humble act of really hearing diverse perspectives can guide our activism towards inclusivity and grassroots engagement.

Above all, cultivating mindful activism might involve allowing ourselves to settle in moments of discomfort. To look beneath the surface of our outrages, our knee-jerk reactions, to sit with our emotions and ask ourselves — why am I moved by this issue? Why does this feel important? These deeply personal, often uncomfortable, reflections are quite literally, where the personal meets the political.

8.4. The Rippling Effects

When the seeds of mindful activism sprout within individuals, they spark a chain reaction that spans across communities, societies, and eventually, transforms into a global impact.

In the personal arena, an increased sense of self-awareness and emotional intelligence betters our interactions with the world around us. Conversations become powerful tools for change; patience, an armour against societal resistance; understanding, the bridge bypassing chasms of difference.

On an organizational level, incorporating mindfulness in activism strategies translates into campaigns that are judged less and listened to more. They offer an inclusive platform that is sensitive to the inputs of every stakeholder, simultaneously fostering environments that are resilient in the face of adversity, yet flexible with the dynamism of societal currents.

At the macro scale, mindful activism has the potential to rewrite global dialogues on justice and representation. It paves the path for nuanced and conscientious policymaking, that is as considerate of humankind's varied narratives, as it is transformative in its reach and efficacy.

"The global impacts of mindful activism are as infinite in their possibility as they are with a conviction for change. They are seeds waiting to sprout into a world that is empathetic and equitable."

In the end, the journey of mindful activism asks of us courage, balance, and the willingness to merge our emotional realities with our larger societal aspirations. Few tasks may seem as grand, but perhaps, therein lies the essence of a meaningful existence — a life lived awake, an activism practised empathetically, and a world changed, one mindful deliberation at a time.

Chapter 9. Sustaining the Momentum: Mindful Strategies for Avoiding Activist Burnout

Mindfulness, a simple yet profound practice of awareness and presence, can serve as an essential tool for sustaining the momentum of social and political activism. In this increasingly chaotic world, the risk of burnout among activists is a critical issue. Activists often expose themselves to emotionally charged situations, and if not managed mindfully, it could lead to spiritual, emotional, and physical exhaustion or burnout. Here, we explore mindful strategies that help avoid such perilous outcomes, sustain momentum, and create enduring change in the social and political landscapes.

9.1. Understanding Activist Burnout

Before delving into ways to prevent activist burnout, it is crucial to understand what it entails. Burnout is a state of chronic physical and emotional exhaustion. For activists, this might amplify as activities involve high emotional investment, with personal values directly woven into the mission. This affliction goes beyond mere tiredness. Activists may experience chronic fatigue, insomnia, and a profound sense of disillusionment and helplessness. It doesn't just affect the body, but the spirit and mental state too, often leading to a diminished sense of accomplishment and cynicism.

9.2. Cultivating Mindfulness and Self-Care

Activism is a marathon, not a sprint. Overexertion of physical and emotional resources without sufficient recovery can lead down the perilous path of burnout. As such, the practice of mindfulness can be particularly effective. Mindfulness can improve emotional resilience, help accept difficult feelings without judgment, and cultivate a greater sense of empathy. Activists can leverage this to manage the emotional burden and maintain their energy levels.

One straightforward practice to cultivate mindfulness is regular meditation. Mindfulness meditation encourages a focus on the current moment, acknowledging and accepting emotions, thoughts, and bodily sensations, thereby helping maintain mental and emotional balance.

In addition to mindfulness, prioritizing self-care is essential. This could comprise a balanced diet, regular exercise, adequate sleep, spending time in nature, or engaging in hobbies. Remember, you cannot serve from an empty vessel.

9.3. Building Resilience through Mindfulness

Given the stressful nature of activism, building resilience is central to avoiding activist burnout. Mindfulness plays a crucial role here. By helping develop a more profound awareness of one's emotions, mindfulness allows activists to navigate high-stress situations more effectively.

Mindfulness-based stress reduction (MBSR) is a useful technique. It combines mindfulness meditation, body awareness, and yoga to help individuals cope with stress. Incorporating such practices in daily life can enhance resilience through improved mental clarity, emotional intelligence, and the ability to maintain calm in the face of adversity.

9.4. Nurturing Community Mental Health

Mindfulness practice isn't confined to self-care. It extends to community care as well. Sharing the burden, seeking help where necessary, and mutual care can be powerful tools to sustain momentum. Building a support network of like-minded individuals enables shared understanding, mutual encouragement, and empathy—bolstering collective resilience.

9.5. Mindful Activism: The Future of Social Change

Building mindfulness into activism prompts a shift in our approach to social change. It asks us to extend empathy, intentionality, and compassion through every action—an approach that can lead to sustainable, long-term changes. Mindful activism fosters healing in the process of fighting for justice.

It is crucial to remember that avoiding activist burnout isn't merely about self-preservation. It is about preserving a movement and, ultimately, humanity. Amid the tumult of social and political activism, mindfulness serves as an anchor—a tool to remain grounded, sustain momentum, and steer change.

While this chapter provides an exhaustive look at the relationship between mindfulness and avoiding activist burnout, it's essential to remember that each activist's journey is personal. Individual needs, personal histories, immediate environments, and contexts will invariably impact their path and approach. Hence, finding what works best for oneself and adapting strategies to personal circumstances is paramount.

The journey towards mindful activism is not easy. It requires constant vigilance and continuous work. Mindfulness, patience, and forgiveness for ourselves and others will be key. It's a journey marked by the satisfaction of fighting for what is right and warm compassion towards humanity—the beautiful intersection of justice and joy.

Chapter 10. Case Studies: Where Mindfulness Meets the Real World of Activism

There is an increasing discourse in various nooks and corners of the world highlighting the intersection of mindfulness and political activism. It may seem at first glance that these two realms are worlds apart, yet upon closer inspection, their intersection unveils a profound symbiosis. What we are witnessing now is a simultaneous movement towards global change and inward transformation. Mindfulness in this context is not a passive, navel-gazing task but, quite the contrary, it is an active, aware, and deeply engaged way of being.

10.1. Case Study One: Mindfulness in Pro-democracy Movements

Over the last few years, we've seen a growing trend of pro-democracy movements integrating mindfulness into their strategies. In Hong Kong, amidst the tumultuous 2019 protests, mindfulness came to the fore as an essential tool for the demonstrators. A striking example is the "Be Water" movement, inspired by martial artist and philosopher Bruce Lee's teachings. The movement embraced the concept of fluidity, adapting and changing shape according to the conditions, much like water does.

For these activists, mindfulness was not just about sitting in silence but about cultivating an acute awareness of their environment, understanding the forces at play, assessing the risks, and making real-time decisions in a volatile situation. It shaped their resilience, focus, and strategic adaptability.

10.2. Case Study Two: Mindfulness in Environmental Activism

The field of environmental activism presents another exciting frontier where mindfulness practices have yielded significant impact. An inspiring example is that of Earth Guardians, a youth-led organization dedicated to environmental preservation and climate justice. Through its revolutionary approach, Earth Guardians use mindfulness to generate an empathetic connection with the natural world.

Guided by Xiuhtezcatl Martinez, Earth Guardians combine mindfulness with direct action and education. Activists are taught to ground their actions in a deep awareness of their thoughts, emotions, and their interconnectedness with the planet. Far from the stereotype of aggressive, combative activism, these environmental stewards show us a way forward marked by peacefulness, compassion, and strategic planning grounded in mindfulness.

10.3. Case Study Three: Mindfulness in Racial Justice Movements

Another arena where mindfulness is playing an increasingly significant role is the racial justice movement. An outstanding example of this dynamic can be seen in the work of Rev. angel Kyodo williams, a Zen priest, activist, and the author of "Radical Dharma: Talking Race, Love, and Liberation."

For Rev. williams, mindfulness is an integral part of activism. It fuels individual and collective change by creating a space where activists can explore their personal and collective histories of racial trauma. There, they can acknowledge, work through their pain, and transform it into compassionate action.

10.4. Case Study Four: Mindfulness in Gender and LGBTQ+ Rights Movements

The Gender and LGBTQ+ rights movements are increasingly aware of the importance of mindfulness to address both internalized and systemic oppression. The practice of mindfulness meditation serves as a powerful tool for activists to increase self-awareness, foster empathy, handle stress, and develop resilience.

A primary example is the Mindfulness-Based Gender Transition (MBGT) program established by Trish Grbich, an experienced therapist and mindfulness teacher, in Melbourne, Australia. The program aims to support individuals in their transition and manage the emotional roller coaster that can come with it. The MBGT program showcases the power of mindfulness in providing a compassionate space for self-exploration and personal growth.

In conclusion, these case studies serve as testaments to an emerging paradigm of activism, one infused with conscious awareness and a steadfast presence. By embracing mindfulness, activists are becoming more attuned to their strengths, more resilient in the face of adversity, and more capable of effecting real, sustainable change. By redefining our understanding of activism–from a solely external act affecting societal structures to an internal journey cultivating self-awareness and compassion–we are standing at the threshold of a promising new era for social change.

Chapter 11. Into the Future: The Potential of Mindful Activism in the Coming Years

In a world increasingly characterized by turmoil and transition, the advent of mindful activism is not just a hopeful emergence – it's a necessity. Mindful activism seeks to reshape the conventional model of activism, balancing the fires of passion and justice with equanimity and consciousness of the present moment.

We will unearth the potential of this transformative approach, as well as its implications in the wider sociopolitical landscape in the years to come. Buckle in, for the road is long and winding, but the destination promises insight and inspiration.

11.1. The Role of Mindful Activism

Mindfulness and activism might seem schismatic at first glance—after all, the calm tranquillity often associated with mindfulness seems far removed from the zealous urgency of activism. Yet, upon closer examination, it's evident these two realms are not only compatible but symbiotic.

Mindful activism invokes qualities of presence, compassion, and interconnectedness to enrich our pursuit of social and political change. It seeks not to quell the fires of passion or dilute the intensity of activism, but rather apply it with intention and focus. Through nurturing calmness amidst the chaos, mindful activists foster resilience and sustainability, preventing burnout and disillusionment so prevalent in traditional activism.

Looking ahead, the role of mindful activism in shaping a more considerate, justice-oriented society appears promising. Recognizing the interconnectedness of all beings fosters empathy, encouraging activists to consider the viewpoints of those they disagree with instead of entrenching themselves further in their pre-existing ideologies. This could pave the way for more constructive debates, reducing polarization, and enabling shared progress.

11.2. Synergizing Inner and Outer Transformations

An essential facet to understand as we journey into the future of mindful activism is the synergy between personal and societal evolution. Mindfulness is traditionally understood as a path to individual enlightenment—cultivating a deepened awareness of the self to foster peace and compassion. However, when integrated with activism, it introduces an interdependence between personal change and societal progress.

The central philosophy in mindful activism is that the outer world is a reflection of our inner states. Individual transformation—achieved through increased mindfulness, awareness, compassion, and justice-oriented thought—can catalyze shifts on a societal level. Conversely, a soulful engagement in societal activism can accelerate personal growth, resulting in a self-perpetuating cycle of transformation.

In the years to come, this interplay between personal and societal transformations may present several intriguing possibilities. For example, as mindfulness practices become mainstream, we could see a rise in conscious policymaking, leading to more socially and environmentally sustainable decisions.

11.3. Tackling Complex Challenges Mindfully

The structural challenges we face, as a society, are increasingly intricate and interconnected—not amenable to simplistic, one-dimensional solutions. Climate change, social inequality, racial discrimination—these are not distinct problems but rather nodes in an interconnected web of discord.

Mindful activism, with its emphasis on interconnectedness and holistic thinking, could offer novel approaches to these complex challenges. Through fostering more nuanced perspectives and encouraging systems thinking, mindful activists can illuminate the underlying drivers of these issues and cultivate solutions that address the root causes rather than just the symptoms.

As we move towards the future, we can expect to see more of these systemic and interconnected solutions emerging from the domain of mindful activism. This approach could be instrumental in fostering new paths toward egalitarian, sustainable societies.

11.4. Fostering Sustainable Activism

Activism is a demanding pursuit—both physically and emotionally. Traditional models of activism often overlook this toll, unwittingly fostering a culture of unsustainable self-sacrifice, leading to eventual burnout. However, in mindful activism, self-care and inner balance are not corners you can cut— they're central to the process.

In the future, mindful activism is poised to rewrite the narrative of what it means to be an activist. Rather than being viewed solely as tireless fighters, activists could be seen as balanced agents of change, who engage in persistent but sustainable activism. This mindset shift can make activism more accessible and resilient, encouraging a greater number of people to participate in social change.

To summarize, the horizon of mindful activism is promising, teeming with potential to reshape our sociopolitical landscape. By fostering awareness, empathy, and interconnectedness, mindful activism could seed a paradigm shift in how we tackle societal challenges. This intersection of inner tranquility and societal urgency might be the elixir our world needs, as we traverse through turbulent times towards a more serene and just future.